The Wrecking Light

Robin Robertson is from the north-east coast of Scotland. He has published three previous collections, *A Painted Field* (1997), *Slow Air* (2002) and *Swithering* (2006), and has received a number of awards for his work, including the E. M. Forster Award from the American Academy of Arts and Letters and all three Forward Prizes – most recently the 2009 Prize for Best Single Poem, for 'At Roane Head'.

ROBIN ROBERTSON

The
Wrecking
Light

PICADOR

First published 2010 by Picador

First published in paperback 2010 by Picador
an imprint of Pan Macmillan, a division of Macmillan Publishers Limited
Pan Macmillan, 20 New Wharf Road, London N1 9RR
Basingstoke and Oxford
Associated companies throughout the world
www.panmacmillan.com

ISBN 978-0-330-51548-1

3 5 7 9 8 6 4

A CIP catalogue record for this book is available from
the British Library.

Printed in Great Britain by CPI Mackays, Chatham ME5 8TD

Visit www.picador.com to read more about all our books
and to buy them. You will also find features, author interviews and
news of any author events, and you can sign up for e-newsletters
so that you're always first to hear about our new releases.

for Janet and John Banville

I dropped it, I dropped it,
and on my way I dropped it

CONTENTS

I

II

III

I
SILVERED WATER

ALBUM

I am almost never there, in these
old photographs: a hand
or shoulder, out of focus; a figure
in the background,
stepping from the frame.
I see myself, sometimes, in the restless
blur of a child, that flinch
in the eye, or the way
sun leaks its gold into the print;
or there, in that long white gash
across the face of the glass
on the wall behind. That
smear of light
the sign of me, leaving.

Look closely
at these snapshots, all this
Kodacolor going to blue, and you'll
start to notice. When you finally see me,
you'll see me everywhere: floating
over crocuses, sandcastles,
fallen leaves, on those
melting snowmen, their faces
drawn in coal – among all
the wedding guests,
the dinner guests, the birthday-
party guests – this smoke
in the emulsion, the flaw.
A ghost is there; the ghost gets up to go.

SIGNS ON A WHITE FIELD

The sun's hinge on the burnt horizon
has woken the sealed lake,
leaving a sleeve of sound. No wind,
just curved plates of air
re-shaping under the trap-ice,
straining to give; the groans and rumbles
like someone shifting heavy tables far below.
I snick a stone over the long sprung deck
to get the dobro's glassy note, the crying
slide of a bottleneck, its
tremulous ululation to the other shore.
The rocks are ice-veined; the trees
swagged with snow.
Here and there, a sudden frost
has caught some turbulence in the water
and made it solid: frozen in its distress
to a scar, or a skin-graft.
Everywhere, frost-heave has jacked up boulders
clear of the surface, and the ice-shove
has piled great slabs on the lake-edge
like luggage tumbled from a carousel.

A racket of jackdaws, the serrated call
of a falcon as I walk out onto the lake.

A living lens of ice; you can hear it bending,
breathing, re-adjusting its weight and light
as the hidden tons of water
swell and stretch underneath,
thickening with cold.

A low grumble, a lingering vibrato, creaks
that seem to echo back and forth for hours;
the lake is talking to itself. A loud
twang in the ice. Twitterings
in the railway lines
from a train about to arrive.
A pencilled-in silence,
hollow and provisional.
And then it comes.
The detonating crack, like a dropped plank,
as if the whole lake has snapped in two
and the world will follow.
But all that happens
is a huge release of sound: a boom
that rolls under the ice for miles,
some fluked leviathan let loose
from centuries of sleep, trying to push through,
shaking the air like sheet metal,
like a muffled giant drum.

I hear the lake all night as a distant war.
In the morning's brightness
I brush the snow off with a glove,
smooth down a porthole in the crust
and find, somehow, the living green beneath.
The green leaf looks back, and sees
a man walking out in this shuddering light
to the sound of air under the ice,
out onto the lake, among sun-cups,
snow penitents: a drowned man, waked
in this weathering ground.

BY CLACHAN BRIDGE

for Alasdair Roberts

I remember the girl
with the hare-lip
down by Clachan Bridge,
cutting up fish
to see how they worked;
by morning's end her nails
were black red, her hands
all sequined silver.
She unpuzzled rabbits
to a rickle of bones;
dipped into a dormouse
for the pip of its heart.
She'd open everything,
that girl.
They say they found
wax dolls in her wall,
poppets full of human hair,
but I'd say they're wrong.
What's true is
that the blacksmith's son,
the simpleton,
came down here once
and fathomed her.
Claimed she licked him
clean as a whistle.
I remember the tiny stars
of her hands around her belly

as it grew and grew, and how
after a year, nothing came.
How she said it was still there,
inside her, a stone-baby.
And how I saw her wrists
bangled with scars
and those hands flittering
at her throat,
to the plectrum of bone
she'd hung there.
As to what happened
to the blacksmith's boy,
no one knows
and I'll keep my tongue.
Last thing I heard, the starlings
had started
to mimic her crying,
and she'd found how to fly.

TULIPS

Sifting sand in the Starsign Hotel
on 96th and Madison,
trying not to hear the sirens: the heart's
fist, desire's empty hand.
The room awash with its terrible light;
a sky unable to rain. Cradling a glass
of nothing much at all, it's all
come down to this: the electric fan's
stop-start – the stalled, half-circle twist
of draught over the bed; the sea-spill
of sheets, the head in storm. Look
at what's beached here on the night-stand:
a flipped photograph and a silk scarf, a set
of keys. These tulips, loosening in a vase.

THE PLAGUE YEAR

Great elms gesture in the last of the light. I am dying
so slowly you'd hardly notice. What is there left
to trust but this green world and its god,
always returning to life? I stood
all day in the vanishing point; my place
now taken by a white-tailed deer.

*

I go to check the children, who are done for.
They lie there broken on their beds, limbs thrown out
in the attitudes of death, the shape of soldiers.
The next morning, I look up at my reflection
in the train window: unshaven, with today's paper;
behind me stands a gunman in a hood.

*

The chestnut trees hold out their breaking buds
like lanterns, or wounds, sticky with life. Under the
false-teeth-whistling flight of a wood-pigeon
a thrown wave of starlings rose and sank itself
back into a hedge, in a burst of chatter.
My father in the heart of the hedge, clasping a bible.

*

Rain muscles its way through the gutters
of Selma and Vine. I look north
through the fog at the Hollywood sign,
east to the observatory where tonight,
under a lack of stars,
old men will be fighting with knives.

★

Western Michigan,
on the Pere Marquette
roll-casting for steelhead:
mending my line over a drift of them
stitched into the shadows,
looking for a loophole in the water.

★

Descending a wrought-iron spiral stair, peering
down at the people very far below;
no hand-rail, every
second step rusted away, I'm holding
a suitcase and a full glass of wine,
wearing carpet slippers and a Balenciaga gown.

★

My past stretches from here to there, and back,
leaving me somewhere in the middle
of Shepherd's Bush Green with the winos of '78.
A great year; I remember it well. Hints of petrol,
urine, plane trees; a finish so long you could
sleep out under it. Same faces, different names.

★

Parrots tear out their feathers, whistling Jingle Bells,
cornfields burst into flames, rivers dry
from their source to the sea, snakes sun themselves
as the roads return to tar; puffer fish off the Lizard,
whales in the Thames, the nets heavy
with swordfish, yellowfin, basking shark.

★

Cyclamen under olive trees; sacked tombs, a ruined
moussaka, with chips. Locals on motorbikes
chew pitta bread, stare out at me like sheep,
their wayside shrines to the saints
built better than their houses; at every bend
tin memorials to the crashed dead.

★

I was down here in the playground
with the other adults,
on the roundabouts and swings,
while up on the hill
on the tennis court,
the children were kneeling to be shot.

*

In November, two ring-necked parakeets
eating from apples still hanging
from the apple tree. The dead crow I notice
is just a torn black bin-liner;
at the end of the garden a sand-pit stands up
as a fox, and slopes off.

*

Smoked mackerel, smoked eel, smoked halibut,
smoked reindeer heart, veal pâté, six different kinds
of salmon, Gustav's Sausage, Jansson's Temptation.
Tasting each *ex voto*, I saw the electrodes
in a bucket, the blade, the gaff, the captive bolt,
walking my plate around the stations of the dead.

WONDERLAND

She said her name was Alice,
that she'd studied with the geisha
in Japan, and was trained and able
in the thousand ways of pleasuring a man.
We'd share some shots of whisky
– her favourite brand, *Black Label* –
then she'd knock them back, and drink me
under the table.

THE TWEED

Giving a back-rub
to Hugh MacDiarmid
I felt, through the tweed,
so much tension
in that determined
neck, those little
bony shoulders
that, when it was released,
he simply
stood up and fell over.

ABOUT TIME

In the time it took to hold my breath
and slip under the bathwater
– to hear the blood-thud in the veins,
for me to rise to the surface –
my parents had died,
the house had been sold and now
was being demolished around me,
wall by wall, with a ball and chain.

I swim one length underwater,
pulling myself up on the other side, gasping,
to find my marriage over,
my daughters grown and settled down,
the skin loosening
from my legs and arms
and this heart going
like there's no tomorrow.

FALL FROM GRACE

I cannot look into the clear faces
of mirrors. The black glass of a window
shines back at me its shame

at all the times and all the places
where I pitched my life in shadow,
and couldn't look into the clear faces

where blame now sits: replacing
love and trust with nothing, no
light shining back at me, just shame.

My head's in flames. My mind races
and I try to shut it down. Sometimes, though,
I can't even look into the faces

of flowers: all beauty carries traces
of what I seeded, then buried in this snow
that now shines back at me in shame.

My life a mix of dull disgraces
and watery acclaim, my daughters know
I cannot look into their clear faces;
what shines back at me is shame.

GOING TO GROUND

That smell of over-cooked vegetables
under the cupboard
was a dead mouse; so small a body
it would soon be gone, I said,
dousing the boards with
our daughter's cheap perfume.

Later, you remembered
where you'd smelt that smell before
– that last sweetness, that old
double-act of death and vanity –
a hospital room
where your Trinity friend
was dying of AIDS,
his toes and fingers
starting to rot and go brown,
how he'd sprayed the bed
and his nails
with eau de cologne.

CAT, FAILING

A figment, a thumbed
maquette of a cat, some
ditched plaything, something
brought in from outside:
his white fur stiff and grey,
coming apart at the seams.
I study the muzzle
of perished rubber, one ear
eaten away, his sour body
lumped like a bean-bag
leaking thinly
into a grim towel. I sit
and watch the light
degrade in his eyes.

He tries and fails
to climb to his chair, shirks
in one corner of the kitchen,
cowed, denatured, ceasing to be
anything like a cat,
and there's a new look
in those eyes
that refuse to meet mine
and it's the shame of being
found out. Just that.
And with that
loss of face
his face, I see,
has turned human.

A GIFT

She came to me in a dress
of true-love and blue rocket,
with fairy-thimbles of foxglove
at the neck and wrist,
in her hair she wore a garland
of cherry laurel, herb bennet,
dwayberries and yew-berries,
twined with stems of clematis,
and at her throat she'd threaded
twists of bryony stalk, seeds
of meadow saffron and laburnum,
linked simply in a necklace,
and she was holding out
a philtre of water lovage,
red chamomile and ladies' seal
in a cup, for me to drink.

STRINDBERG IN BERLIN

All the wrong turnings
that have brought me here –
debts, divorce, a court trial, and now
a forced exile in this city and this drinking cell,
Zum schwarzen Ferkel, The Black Piglet:
neither home nor hiding-place, just
another indignity,
just a different make of hell.

Outside, a world of people queuing
to stand in my light, and that sound
far in the distance, of my life
labouring to catch up.
I've now pulled out
every good tooth
in search of the one that was making me mad.
I squint at the flasks and alembics,
head like a wasps' nest,
and pour myself
three fingers and a fresh start.
A glass of *aqua vitae*, a straightener,
stiffener, a universal tincture – same again –
the great purifier, clarifier,
a steadying hand on the dancing hand,
– one more, if you wouldn't mind –
bringer of spirit and the spirit of love;
the cleansing fire, turning lead
to gold, the dead back into life.

The Pole at the piano, of course;
Munch opposite me, his face
like a shirt done up wrong.
My fiancée in one corner, my lover in another,
merging, turning, as all women turn,
back into my daughters,
and I am swimming naked at night,
off the island, in the witch-fire of *mareld* light,
listening to the silence of the stars,
with my children beside me,
my beautiful lost children, in the swell
of the night, swimming beside me.

And back, to the bright salts and acids,
the spill and clamour of the bar,
the elixirs, the women:
my wife-to-be, my young lover –
one banked hearth, one unattended fire.
Christ. The hot accelerant of drink.
The rot of desire.
And out, out into the swinging dark,
a moon of mercury, lines of vitriol trees
and the loose earth that rises up,
drops on me, burying me,
night after night after night.

VENERY

What is he to think now,
the white scut
of her bottom
disappearing
down the half-flight
carpet stair
to the bathroom?
What is he to do
with this masted image?
He put all his doubt
to the mouth of her long body,
let her draw the night
out of him like a thorn.
She touched it, and it moved: that's all.

MY GIRLS

How many times
have I lain alongside them
willing them to sleep
after the same old stories;
face to face, hand in hand,
till they smooth into dream and I can
slip these fingers free
and drift downstairs:
my face a blank,
hands full of deceit.

TINSEL

Tune to the frequency of the wood and you'll hear
the deer, breathing; a muscle, tensing; the sigh
of a fieldmouse under an owl. Now

listen to yourself – that friction – the push-and-drag,
the double pulse, the drum. You can hear it, clearly.
You can hear the sound of your body, breaking down.

If you're very quiet, you might pick up loss: or rather
the thin noise that losing makes – *perdition*.
If you're absolutely silent

and still, you can hear nothing
but the sound of nothing: this voice
and its wasting, the soul's tinsel. Listen ... Listen ...

LEAVING ST KILDA

Clouds stream over the edge of Mullach Mòr, pouring
into the valley as we sail against the sun from Village Bay,
rounding the Point, and the Point of the Water,
north under Oiseval and the Hill of the Wind, and round
past the Skerry of the Cormorants, the Cleft
of the Sea-Shepherd, and out around the Yellow Headland
to The Hoof, and the Cleft of the Hoof, to The Gap
where the fulmars nest in their sorrel and chickweed;
and on to Stac a'Langa, the Long Stack
also called the Stack of the Guillemot, and Sgeir Dhomnuill,
place of shags, who are drying their wings like a line
of blackened tree-stumps, to Mina Stac and Bradastac
under the deep gaze of Conachair the Roarer
and Mullach Mòr the Great Summit,
and the White Summit and the Bare Summit beyond;
from there to the Cleft of the Leap, of the Ruinous Fall,
and round the promontory, and its tunnels and arches
to Geò nan Plaidean, the Cleft of the Blankets,
and Geò nan Ròn, the Cleft of the Seals, to rest
by Hardship Cave and the deep doorways in the cliffs
of wide Glen Bay; the air still, the Atlantic flat as steel.
Southwards lies Gleann Mòr, the Great Glen, which holds
the Brae of Weepings, the House of the Trinity
and The Amazon's House, The Well of Many Virtues,
and also, it's said, above The Milking Stone, among
the shielings, a place they call The Plain of Spells.
Here also, the home of the great skua,
the bonxie, the harasser: pirate, fish-stealer,
brown buzzard of the sea who kills for the sake of it.

And on past the Cleft of the Lame and the Beach of the Cairn
of the Green Sword and the Chasm of the Steep Skerry
to the crest of The Cambir, and round its ridge to Soay.

Three great sea-stacks guard the gateway to the Isle of Sheep:
the first, Soay Stac, the second, Stac Dona – also called
The Stack of Doom – where nothing lives. The third – kingdom
of the fulmar, and tester of men who would climb
her sheer sides – the Pointed Stack, Stac Biorach.
Out on the ocean, they ride the curve of the wave; but here
in the air above their nests, in their thousands, they are ash
blown round a bonfire, until you see them closer, heeling
and banking. The grey keel
and slant of them: shearing,
planing the rock, as if their endless
turning of it might shape the stone –
as the sea has fashioned the overhangs
and arches, pillars, clefts and caves, through
centuries of close attention, of making its presence known.
Under the stacks, the shingle beach at Mol Shoay,
filled with puffins, petrels, shearwaters, and on the slopes
up to The Altar, the brown sheep of Soay graze.
Above the cliffs, and round again past the Red Cleft
to the rocks of Creagan, Am Plaistir, the Place of Splashing,
under the grey hill of Cnoc Glas, to the Point of the Strangers,
the Point of the Promontory, Flame Point, and beyond that
the Skerry of the Son of the King of Norway.

Back to Hirta and The Cambir to the Mouth of the Cleft
and The Cauldron Pool and down through the skerries
to the western heights of Mullach Bi – the Pillar Summit –

and Claigeann Mòr, Skull Rock.
Between them, the boulder field of Carn Mòr – sanctuary
of storm petrels, Leach's petrels, Manx shearwaters –
and up on the ridge, the Lover's Stone.
Past The Beak of the Wailer, Cleft of the Grey Cow,
the Landing Place of the Strangers, to An Torc, The Boar,
rising from the sea under Mullach Sgar and Clash na Bearnaich,
and The Notches that sit under Ruaival
the Red Fell, pink with thrift – past the white churning
at the mouth of the kyle, and on through the mists
of kittiwakes to the serrated fastness of Dùn:
The Doorpost, The Fank, the Lobster Precipice, Hamalan
the Anvil Rock, The Pig's Snout,
The Fissures, and The Beak of Dùn.

And then north-east, four miles, to the fortress of Boreray,
rising a thousand feet out of the black-finned sea.
To the northern stack: Stac an Armin, Stack of the Warrior,
highest sea-stack in these islands of Britain, where the last
great auk was killed as a witch
a hundred and seventy years ago. On its southern edge,
The Spike, Am Biran, and Broken Point – long loomery
of the guillemot – and across to The Heel,
split vertically in two, and the Cleft of Thunder.
Round, then, the heights of Boreray,
clockwise this time, round
to high Sunadal the swimmy-headed, home of puffins,
and the village of cleits
like turf-roofed chambered cairns
looking down on the Rock of the Little White Headland,
the Bay of a Woman, the Point of the Dale of the Breast,

and round the southern tip of Boreray, Gob Scapanish
– Headland of the Sheaths, Point of the Point of Caves –
and Cormorant Rock and The Cave of Ruin and then
Clagan na Rùsgachan, Skull Rock of the Fleeces,
wreathed in banner-clouds,
the Chasm of the Warrior and the great rift of Clesgor
– to reach, in the west, the Grey Stack, the Hoary Rock,
the gannetry of St Kilda: Stac Lee.
From one side a bishop's piece, from another, a shark;
all sides inches deep with guano you can smell for miles.
A stone hive of gannets, thrumming and ticking
with the machinery of sixty thousand squalling birds.
Off the rock, they open out in perfect cruciform and glide
high over the deep swell to track the shadows
of the mackerel or the herring shoal and then,
from a hundred feet, hundreds of them drop:
folding their wings
to become white javelins –
the dagger bill,
the pointed yellow head,
white body,
white wings tipped black –
they crash
white
into their own white water.

*

All eyes stay fixed
on the great sea-citadel, this
mountain range returning to the waves,

all eyes hold the gaze of the rocks
as the boat turns east – as if
to look away would break the spell –
until a shawl of mist
goes round its shoulders,
the cloud-wreaths
close over it, and it's gone.

At last we turn away, and see them
leading us: bow-riding dolphins,
our grey familiars,
and thirty gannets in a line
drawing straight from Boreray:
a gannet guard
for this far passage,
for the leaving of St Kilda.

II
BROKEN WATER

LAW OF THE ISLAND

They lashed him to old timbers
that would barely float,
with weights at the feet so
only his face was out of the water.
Over his mouth and eyes
they tied two live mackerel
with twine, and pushed him
out from the rocks.

They stood, then,
smoking cigarettes
and watching the sky,
waiting for a gannet
to read that flex of silver
from a hundred feet up,
close its wings
and plummet-dive.

KALIGHAT

Only a blue string tethers him to the present.
The small black goat; the stone enclosure;
the forked wooden altar washed in coconut
milk, hung with orange and yellow marigolds;
the heap of sodden sand.
With a single bleat
he folds himself into a shadow in the corner,
nosing a red hibiscus flower onto its back
and nibbling the petals.
The temple bells; the drum. It is nearly time.
A litre of Ganges holy water
up-ended over him. He's dragged
shivering to centre-stage and
slotted, white-eyed, into place. On the last
drumbeat, the blade separates
his head from his body. The blood
comes out of his neck
in little gulps.
The tongue and eyes are still
moving in the head
as the rest of him
is thrown down next to it.
Neither of his two parts can quite take this in.
The legs go on trembling,
pedalling at the dirt – slowly trying to drag
the body back to its loss: the head
on its side, dulling eyes fixed
on this black, familiar ghost;
its limbs flagging now,

the machinery running down.
There's some progress, but not enough, then
after a couple of minutes, none at all.
The last thing I notice is a red petal
still in his mouth, and another,
six inches away, in his throat.

RELIGION

after Bonfire Night
I find christ in the fields:
the burst canister

its incense heavy
in the coloured cardboard tube:
asperged, bright with dew

PENTHEUS AND DIONYSUS

after Ovid

Pentheus – man of sorrows, king
of Thebes – despised the gods, and had no time
for blind old men or their prophecies.
'You're a fool, Tiresias, and you belong
in the darkness. Now, leave me be!'
'You might wish, sire, for my affliction soon enough,
if only to save you from witnessing
the rites of Dionysus.
He is near at hand, I feel it now,
and if you fail to honour him – your cousin
the god – you will be torn to a thousand ribbons
left hanging in the trees, your blood
fouling your mother and her sisters.
Your eyes have sight but you are blind.
My eyes are blind but I see the truth . . . '

But before Tiresias had finished with his warning,
even as the king pushed him away,
it had already begun.

He was walking on the earth,
and you could hear the shrieks
of the dancers in the fields, see the people
streaming out of the city, men and women,
young and old, nobles and commoners, climbing
to Cithaeron and the god
who was now made manifest.

Pentheus stared out in disbelief.
'What lunacy is this? You people
bewitched by cymbals, pipes and trickery –
you who have stood with swords drawn
in the din of battle on the field of war –
now dance with a gaggle of wailing women
waving tambourines? You wear garlands
instead of helmets, hold fennel wands
instead of spears – and all for some boy!
If the walls of Thebes were to fall
– which they will not – it would be
at the hands of soldiers and their engines of war,
not by the flowers, the embroidered robes
and scented hair of this weaponless pretty-boy.
Find him! Bring him here, where he'll
confess that he's no son of Zeus and these
sacred rites are just a shaman's lie.
Bring him here to me now, in chains!'

His counsellors gathered, muttering restraint,
which just inflamed the king
who, like a river in spate,
boiled and foamed
at any hindrance in the way.

His men returned, stained in blood,
claiming they saw no sign
of Dionysus, just this priest of his
– a comrade and an acolyte – and they
pushed forward the man, a foreigner,

hands tied behind his back.
Eyes bright with rage, Pentheus
spoke slowly:
'Before you die, I want your name,
your country, and why you came here with this
fraud and his filthy cult.'
Unblinking, the prisoner replied:
'I am Acoetes, from Lydia,
son of a humble fisherman,
now a fisherman myself.
I learnt how to steer, to set a course,
to read the wind and stars,
so I left the rocks of home and went to sea.
I'd raised a crew, and on our way to Delos
a storm forced a landfall
on the shores of Chios. The next morning
I sent the men to fetch fresh water
and they came back with a child.
The bosun pulled him up on board, saying
they'd found him in a field, this prize,
this boy as beautiful as a girl, stumbling
slightly from sleep, or wine.
I knew, by the face, by every movement,
that this was no mortal,
that I was looking at a god.
"Honour this child," I said to the crew,
"for he is not of us." And to the boy:
"Show us grace and bless our labours
and grant these men forgiveness,
for they know not what they do."
The lookout slid down the rigging, calling

"Don't you bother with prayers on our account,"
and the others circled, nodding and shouting,
their voices fat with greed.
"I am the captain, and I'll have no
sacrilege aboard this ship, and no
harm to our fellow traveller."
"Our *plunder*," said the worst of them
taking me by the throat
to the cheers and yelps of the rest.
And their noise woke Dionysus – for it was him
who opened his eyes –
"Tell me sailors: what's happening?
How did I get here and where am I going?"
One told him not to worry, asked him
to name his port of call.
"Naxos. Turn your course for Naxos,
my home, and you'll find a welcome there."
And so the mutinous crew
swore by all the gods of the sea they would do
just that and told me to set sail.
Naxos lay to starboard but
winking and laughing
they made me steer to port.
"I'll have no hand in this," I said,
and I was shouldered from the helm.
"No one is indispensable, captain.
We'll make our own luck now."
And the painted prow was turned
away from Naxos, out to the open sea.

Then the god began to toy with them.
Gazing out from the curving deck

across the ocean, feigning tears, he cried:
"These are not the shores you promised me,
these shores are not my home.
What glory is there when men
deceive a boy – so many against one?"
My tears were real, but the mutineers
just laughed at both of us and kept on rowing.

Now I swear to you by that god himself
– and there is no god nearer than him –
that this is true: that the ship just stopped.
It stood still on the sea as if in dry dock.
The panicked men pulled harder,
letting out sail to try and find the wind,
but ivy was swarming up the oars
twining tendrils round the blades,
whipping along the decks and up the mast,
dragging at the encumbered sails
till they sagged in heavy-berried clusters.
And now the god revealed himself at last.
Around his brow a garland of grapes;
in his hand a wand, tight-twisted with vine;
and at his feet, the slinking
phantom shapes of wild beasts:
tigers, lynxes, panthers.

Illusions, perhaps, but the crew began to leap
overboard, in terror or madness or both.
One body darkened and went black,
back lifting in a curve; another started to call out
just as his jaws spread wide, his nose hooked over,
his skin hardened into scales. Another, still

fumbling with an oar, looked down
and saw his hands shrinking till they were
hands no more, just fins.
And I watched one, reaching up for a rope, finding
he had no arms
and as he toppled over,
finding he had no legs either:
all torso, he back-flipped into the sea,
with a tail horned like a crescent moon.
They leapt on every side in showers of spray:
bursting free of the water, plunging down again
like dancers or tumblers turning through the air.

The only human left of twenty
I stood there shaking
till I heard the god speak out:
"Hold your nerve
and this empty ship
and track us down the coast to home!"
And so I did. And there I joined
his rites and sacrifices, and now I follow him:
Iacchus, Bromius, Liber, Dionysus.'

'Well,' said Pentheus, 'I have listened patiently
to this rambling fantasy of yours:
an attempt, no doubt, to diminish my anger
and delay your punishment. Well, it didn't work.
Take him, men, and break him on the rack.
Send him down to Hell.'
And so Acoetes was dragged away
to the cells; but while the fire, the steel,

the instruments of pain, were being prepared
the studded doors flew open of their own accord
and the forged chains fell from his hands.

Hearing this – not trusting anyone now –
Pentheus stood and went
to settle things, once and for all.
Alone, he clambered up Cithaeron, the mountain
chosen for these rites, now ringing
with the songs and chants of the maenads,
the celebrants of the god.
And he was stirred by them, roused like a warhorse
at the sound of battle trumpets, their
shiver in the air. The long cries
thrilling through him
he pressed on:
skittish, fevered, feeling again
some passion in him flare.

Halfway up the mountainside,
surrounded by woods, was an open clearing.
Here he stood, in full view. Here he looked
upon the naked mysteries with uninitiated eyes.
The first to see him, the first
to rush at him, the first
to hurl her sharpened wand into his side,
was Agave, his mother,
screaming: 'Come, my sisters, quick!
There is a wild boar here we must kill!'
And the three sisters led the rest
and fell on him in frenzy,

and Pentheus the king was terrified, crying out,
confessing all his sins. Blood
streaming from a hundred wounds
he called to Autonoë: 'I am Pentheus!
Don't you know your own nephew?
Would you do to me
what the dogs did to Actaeon, your son?'
But the names meant nothing to her,
and she simply
tore his right arm out of its shoulder.
Her sister, Ino, wrenched off the other
like a pigeon's wing.
With no hands left to pray, no arms
to reach for his mother, he just said,
'Mother, look at me.'
And Agave looked, and howled, and shook
the hair from her face, and went to him
and took his head in her hands
and in a throb of rapture
twisted it, clean off.
In her bloody grip, the head swung
with its red strings: 'See,
my sisters: victory!'
And quicker than a winter wind strips
the last leaves from a tree,
so all the others ripped Pentheus to pieces
with their own bare hands.

By this lesson piety was learned,
and due reverence for the great god Dionysus,
for his rites, and for this holy mountain shrine.

LESSON

The green leaf opens
and the leaf falls,

each breath is a flame
that gives in to fire;

and grief is the price
we pay for love,

and the death of love
the fee of all desire.

THE DAUGHTERS OF MINYAS

after Ovid

Son of Zeus, son of the thunderbolt,
Iacchus the twice-born, child
of the double door, Bromius
the roaring god, the coming one,
the vanishing one, the god
who stands apart; god of frenzy
and release, god of the vine.
The one
of many names and many faces.
The horned god. Young
beyond time.
The god
that changes. The Other.
Dionysus.

*

'And noise, just a lot of noise: drums,
cymbals, flutes – not even music – shouting
and screaming and dancing up the mountain
to kill some goat, no doubt.
And all that blooming *ivy . . .* '

'They say Mount Cithaeron flows with blood . . .'

'Wine, more like.'

'They say the king has gone.
That when the women were done with their play

and finally laid him down
he must have been tired
for his head rolled away like a stone.'

'They're all drunk. I wouldn't believe a word.
Another false god turns up and off they go.
If that pretty boy's a son of Zeus, then I can fly.
Believe me, it will pass.
It's the priests I blame: whipping up this madness.
Our servant girls deserting their tasks –
their looms and basket-work – unbinding their hair
and putting on garlands, carrying those *spear things*,
those fennel stalks tied up with vine leaves,
burning incense – and all of them dressed
in *animal skins*, for heaven's sake.
You won't catch me in some procession
up a mountain with a bunch of stupid girls
because a priest says we should celebrate a god.
Him and his so-called mysteries.
We are the daughters of Minyas
and we have our god – sweet Pallas Athena –
and we don't need a false idol, or his wine.
Let's pass the hours while we spin and weave
by telling stories, and by the time we're done
all will be quiet and everything back to normal.'

'Here's one. About how the mulberry changed
from white to red because of blood.
An Eastern story this, about the handsome Pyramus
and his neighbour, the beautiful Thisbe.
Separated by their parents, and a wall,

each night they kissed the stone that lay between.
They pledged to meet, after dark, by this tomb
with a mulberry bush nearby. Thisbe gets there first,
but is scared off by a lioness all bloody-mouthed
from some ghastly business. She escapes,
but drops her shawl, which the beast tears to pieces.
Then along comes Pyramus, finds the shawl
and thinks she's dead, so kills himself.
Blood everywhere. All over the bush.
Then Thisbe returns, of course, sees her loved one
lying dead, and kills herself. More blood,
and that's why mulberries are red.'

'*Lovely* story, but a bit dull. No sex, at least,
for once; that's a relief.'

'Here's another. It tells how the Sun falls in love.
But before that, we hear how his light sees everything first:
in this case, brightening the bed where Ares lies
entertaining Aphrodite, wife of the fire-god Hephaestus . . . '

'Oh, the cripple? The donkey-rider?'

'The very same – but now *cuckold* too. And so Hephaestus –
who's good with his hands, if nothing else – fashions this
invisible net of bronze, finer than the finest spider's web,
and traps his wife and her lover in the very act.'

'Disgusting. And I suppose the other gods were watching?'

'Of course – which fuelled the shame
of Aphrodite, and stoked her vengeance.'

'Against her gimp of a husband – the blacksmith?'

'No, no: against *the Sun!* She makes him fall in love
with this virgin princess. He turns up in disguise, then
discloses himself to her – you know? And so,
overwhelmed by his radiance, his *magnificence*,
she gives in. As you would.
But there's another girl who also loves the Sun,
and in her jealousy she tells the king,
who's so furious at his daughter's crime
he buries her alive.
The Sun, distraught, tries to save her, but to no avail.
"In spite of Fate," he says, "you'll still reach up to heaven,"
and sprinkles the ground with nectar. Up comes
this shrub of frankincense, stretching to the sky.
The other girl, meanwhile – the jealous one –
is changed into a tiny flower, doomed to turn her face
forever, following the sun.'

'Good. They got what they deserved.'

'Time for one more.
This is the story of the fountain pool whose waters
turn men's bodies soft as girls': home of the nymph
Salmacis, who wouldn't follow Artemis, who chose
the mirror and brush over the javelin and bow.
When a beautiful boy – almost a man – appears
at the pool, she's eaten up by desire and tries
to kiss him, but he's still too young to understand.
She retreats, watching him slip off his clothes and dive in.
Beside herself, she plunges after him, pulling
him under, taking him by force, and praying
to the gods that their bodies will never be parted.
And so it was, like two trees grafted,

they were made one – and that *one*
was neither man nor woman: it was Hermaphroditus.
In his new voice he asked his parents,
Hermes and Aphrodite, to curse this pool forever,
so that any boy who swam in it would be unmanned.
And so it came to be.'

The daughters of Minyas sat in silence, then, for a while.

Eventually, they went back to their work:
taking their minds off the boy in the pool,
the gods in their bed; those mulberries.
They busied themselves with their weaving,
trying to forget what was going on
up on the mountain with all the other women
and their ridiculous prophet. Not wanting
to even think about it (the hard
young bodies and all those wet mouths
turning to feast) they kept their hands moving
and stayed very quiet.

A quiet that was torn open – that moment –
by shrieks, drumbeats, horns, bones
and bells and pipes, the bleating cries
of things unspeakable, the air dense and sweet
with saffron and myrrh; and then,
unbelievably, their weaving turned to green.
Their looms were sudden tents of ivy, twined
and looped with its emerald and jade, the curtains
swagged with fruit, drooping tapestries of vine –
their gold brocade and delicate laces
now swathed in budding creepers, blue-veined leaves.

Each thread became a tendril, their spools
and spindles tightening and thickening to stems,
festooned now with the dark red
flesh and weight of grapes.

The house shuddered into dusk
and all the oil-lamps flared up
and torches spat and smoked
in every room and all around them
grew the shapes and sounds of beasts.
Each sister shirked the light, flinching
from the flames into the deep shadows,
and as they scuttled in corners
a new skin started growing,
stretching from their withered arms
to their shrivelled feet, though they were
too busy flittering there
to notice.
But when they tried to speak their grief,
all that they heard was a tiny
high-pitched squeak.

No human can hear them now
where they hang, huddled in the rafters,
under the thatch.
Shunning our daylight
they flit only by night
and take their name
from the time that they appear:
the vesper bats.

AN AMBUSH

None survived.
The platoon had forgotten
the fable of the patient fox, waiting
for the night's sudden
drop to zero.
A minute is all it takes
and the white lake is dotted in stars
already frozen red,
and the blown feathers of ducks.
Just their feet left
still standing there, webbed hard
into the trap-ice.

ODE TO A LARGE TUNA IN THE MARKET

after Neruda

Here,
among the market vegetables,
this torpedo
from the ocean
depths,
a missile
that swam,
now
lying in front of me
dead

surrounded
by the earth's green froth
– these lettuces,
bunches of carrots.
Only you
lived through
the sea's truth, survived
the unknown, the
unfathomable
darkness, the depths
of the sea,
le grand abîme,
only you:
varnished
black-pitched
witness
to that deepest night.

Only you:
dark bullet
barrelled
from the depths,
carrying only
your one wound,
but renewed,
always resurgent,
locked into the current,
fins fletched
like wings
in the torrent,
in the coursing
of the underwater dark,
like a grieving arrow,
sea-javelin, a nerveless
oiled harpoon.

Dead
in front of me,
catafalqued king
of my own ocean;
once
sappy as a sprung fir
in the green turmoil,
once seed
to sea-quake,
tidal wave, now
simply
dead remains.

In the whole market
yours
was the only shape left
with purpose or direction
in this
jumbled ruin
of nature;
you are armed
amongst this greenery,
a solitary man of war,
your flanks and prow
black
and slippery
as if you were still
a well-oiled ship of the wind,
the only
true
machine
of the sea: unflawed,
undefiled,
navigating now
the waters of death.

GRAVE GOODS

He wanted to outlive the grim husbandry
of battle order, outrun
the breath of the damned, his sleeves
flecked with their spit, his sword with their dung;
to move beyond the hooks and eyes
of women, their insinuated blades, to pass
through the scrim of tissue, through this
chanonry of blood, to reach a place
of peace and honour, fresh running water,
a morning of porcelain and lavender
combed by light, folded and smoothed over.

He came instead to a closed silence. Here
were the attributes and trappings of the hunt:
flint blades and fishhooks, bone pendants,
carved figurines of elk, snakes and humans,
a wild boar's leg-bone whittled and whetted
into a dagger, bear skulls for bowls, stone flakes
for arrowheads. A seated woman with a baby
in her lap, dusted in red ochre, next to a man
wearing a crown of antlers. Between the two,
and dead like them, a young child laid down
into the wing of a swan.

ALBATROSS IN CO. ANTRIM

after Baudelaire

The men would sometimes try to catch one,
throwing a looped wire at the great white cross
that tracked their every turn, gliding over their deep
gulfs and bitter waves: the bright pacific albatross.

Now, with a cardboard sign around his neck, the king
of the winds stands there, hobbled: head shorn,
ashamed; his broken limbs hang down by his side,
those huge white wings like dragging oars.

Once beautiful and brave, now tarred, unfeathered,
this lost traveller is a bad joke; a lord cut down to size.
One pokes a muzzle in his mouth; another limps past,
mimicking the *skliff*, *sclaff* of a bird that cannot fly.

The poet is like this prince of the clouds
who rides the storm of war and scorns the archer;
exiled on the ground, in all this derision,
his giant wings prevent his marching.

THE GREAT MIDWINTER SACRIFICE, UPPSALA

It seems I came too late.
The cart-tracks leading
down the hill to the old town
are frosting over, already filling with snow.
If the temple is gold, as they say,
it's too dark now to tell. I tether my horse
and walk through the ruins of the marketplace,
its stalls empty, the tables of the feast
all cleared; mice among the grain, and dogs,
but few people anywhere.
There's ice between the cobblestones
where drink was spilt – some scraps of bread,
chicken bones – that's it.
I had missed the full moon, and the Festival.
Fires sputter here and there but there is little light
and the ground beyond the square
is frozen hard as iron.
I pass what looks like a well in the darkness
– the sharpening wind playing over it
as you would blow on the neck of an empty bottle.
I hear the creaking of a tree so huge
it's blotted out the moon; some birds, scuffling;
a skitter of rats and a dog's low growl.

As I near the tree I feel the ground soften, start
to suck at my boot-heels, and I can
make out shapes in the high branches:
long, hanging shapes that seem to

turn slightly in the breeze, which is sweet now
beyond the frost, and I almost
sense some drops of rain.
Moving around it
and into the moonlight, I see it's as high
as the temple, fully green, and thick with gifts
the way the peasants dress their beams with corn,
at home, at harvest-time. This tree, though,
is decked simply with the dead.
At the top, what look like cockerels, rams
and goats, then dogs and pigs, and hooked
to the lowest, strongest boughs – their legs
almost touching the earth – horses and bulls.
I count nine of each of them, and nine
that aren't animals but hang there just the same,
black-faced, bletted, barely
recognisable as men.
I look down at the spongy grass
and my boots are soaking red.

My name is Adam of Bremen
and I saw these things
in The Year of Our Lord 1075.

WEB

The wood is hung with silk anchor-
threads and signal-threads. Draglines
catch on my hair and hands, stringing
my face as I move through the trees: strands
charged and sticky as spun sugar
cling and stretch and fizzle apart.
I am ravelled here
to the live field, in a rig of stress.

Turned on my new axis to a swathe
of shriven grey, I remind myself
of a cork float in a fishing-net spread out
to dry in the sun, waiting for the fisherman
– both *retiarius* and *secutor* –
to attend to what is broken and undone.
I watch now as the spider unknots itself
slowly, and elbows out of the dark.

THE HAMMAM

Under the nineteen stars
and the ninety-six minor stars
of the marble heaven,
he lies crossways
on the heated stone,
his laved body evaporating
upwards to the light.

His smoke of sweat condenses
in the dome's stone cupola
and its slow hot rain
drops down on him hard
as annunciation – or nails,
perhaps, on a sheet of tin,
pricking out some finial star.

THE ACT OF DISTRESS

I let him
lose himself in me;
finding a way to sleep,
to disappear
out of darkness and in
to some blue light.

I hear him
sobbing as he
nears the centre, to release
the flare, send up
the high maroon, feel it
flooding the night.

WHITE

It wasn't meant to be that way.
I never expected it to shoot so hard
it blinded me: I'd wanted to watch
the way it went. The pumping-out not like
coming at all, more like emptying
a bottle: blacking out
a little more with every pulse.
I just felt light and very cold at the end,
astonished at how much red there was
and my wrist so white.

III

UNSPOKEN WATER

THE WOOD OF LOST THINGS

We went walks here, as children, listening out
for gypsies, timber wolves, the great
hinges in the trees. Hours
we'd wander its long green halls
making swords from branches,
gathering stars of elderflower
to thread into a chain.
Today the forest sends up birds
to distract me, deer to turn me from the track,
puts out stems and tendrils
to trip and catch at my feet.
The sudden sun opens a path of flowers:
snowdrops, crocuses, hyacinths,
a smoke of bluebells
in the shade on either side;
a way of stamens and stigmas: the breathing
faces of flowers. I look back at the empty trees,
look up at the green, and I'm walking
through daisies and honeysuckle,
fireweed, crab apple, burnt-out
buddleia, a tangle of nettles,
berberis, bramble-wire;
the flowers gone,
just the starred calyx
and the green ovary
hardening to seed.
I take a last look at the yellow trees,
a last look at the brown, and I hear the sound
of old leaves under my feet
and the low noise of water.

I have found the place I wasn't meant to find.
The shallow creek, churning
its red and silver secrets:
failed salmon, bearded with barbs,
riding each other down;
the shore lined with baby pigeons, animals
birthing, others coming back to die.
Placenta and bones in the undergrowth,
in the clearing, in the places of drowning.
Jellyfish have taken to the woods;
mussels rope the tree-trunks.
I watch a fish flip on a thorn
in a pester of flies, one eye fixed on mine.

The wood stretched behind me, now full
of my own kind, those
who have stepped through my shadow;
a life's-worth of women in the forest corridor,
faces turned to the bark. The rows of lovers.
Mother and sister. Wife. And my daughters,
walking away into the blue distance,
turning their heads to look back.

Hung on a silver birch, my school cap
and satchel; next to them, the docken suit,
and next to that, pinned to a branch,
my lost comforter –
a piece of blanket worn to the size of my hand.
My hand as a boy. The forgotten smell of it,
the smell of myself.

And something is moving, something
held down by stones, and one by one
I see the dead unbury themselves
and take their places by the seated corpse
whose face I seem to know.
He was shivering. *It's cold*, I said.
He looked up at me and nodded, *It's cold*.
What is this place? What brings you here?
This is my home, we replied.

MIDDLE WATCH, HAMMERSMITH

He switches off the fridge
just to sit and watch
the hardness of the iced-up
ice-box start to drip,
its white block
loosening like a tooth.

LANDFALL

The fishboxes
of Fraserburgh, Aberdeen,
Peterhead, the wood that broke
on your beach, crates that once held herring,
freshly dead, now hold distance, nothing but the names
of the places I came from, years ago;
and you pull me from the waves,
drawing me out like a skelf,
as I would say:
a splinter.

CALLING HOME

after Tomas Tranströmer

Our phonecall spilled out into the dark
and glittered between the countryside and the town
like the mess of a knife-fight.
Afterwards, all night jittery and spent in the hotel bed,
I dreamt I was the needle in a compass
some orienteer bore through the forest with a spinning heart.

ICTUS

for Tomas Tranströmer

I find myself at your side, turning the pages
for you – haltingly – with my wrong hand,
while you play those delicate, certain notes
without effort, sounding a long
free line through the sea-lanes on the skiff
of *your* wrong hand, the left,
your only moving hand,
your whole right side snowbound.

Who would swap the hammer
for the hammer-blow, the seasons
for this wintering life, that
lethal fold in time? No one I know.
But there are those who can make an art
of setting a logan-stone rocking
here in Södermalm, or learn the perfect
stress of lines, and ferry-times, by heart.

I find I can suddenly read the score, know
when to turn the page: cack-handed,
my dull heart-tick always indicating left.
Sunlight squares the room
and I am snowblind. You slip away
on the wind. Your grandfather,
the pilot, stares out over the archipelago
from his solid wooden frame.

THE UNWRITTEN LETTER

after Montale

Only this? Those shivers at first-light, this succession
of moments, thread after thin thread – hours, years
drawn into the curve of a life – is this it? That pair
of dolphins, circling with their young, do they only
leap and tumble for a few hours, a few days? No,
I don't want to hear from you,
don't want to see your eyes.
There's more to life than this.

I can't dive, can't reappear; night's red
pyrotechnics are running late, the evening drags,
all prayer is hopeless, the message
in its bottle hasn't made it through the rocks.
The empty waves smash open
on the point at Finisterre.

BEGINNING TO GREEN

I find a kind of hope here, in this
homelessness, in this place
where no one knows me –
where I'll be gone, like some
over-wintering bird,
before they even notice.

Healed by distance
and a landscape opening
under broken sun, I like this
mirror-less, flawless world
with no people in it,
only birds.

Unmissed, I can see myself again
in this great unfurling – the song,
the fledged leaf, the wing;
in these strong trees that
twist from the bud: their grey
beginning to green.

DURING DINNER

for Beatrice Monti della Corte

I tried to tell the Baronessa
she shouldn't cut the *biancospino*
and certainly never bring it here indoors.
In my country you fetch
death into the house with hawthorn, I cried;
but seeing I hadn't impressed her
with my folklore, tried again.
Better to leave it, wild,
standing like smoke in the olive groves
or in the hanging valley down below,
than set it on the dresser
and give us all bad luck.
Then, changing tack:
It was Christ's crown and the faeries' bed,
I said to my hostess, my poor confessor,
getting her attention back,
but 'Ladies' Meat' is another name
because it smells of sex and it smells of death.
Then brilliantly I second-guessed her:
For years I was only able to smell one.
Now I can only smell the other!
And with that – heaven bless her –
she rose, and left the table.

ARSENIO

after Montale

The wind-devils stir up the dust
and swirl over the roof-tops, waltzing
down the empty driveways
of all the grand hotels, where the horses
stand, hooded and stock-still
by the blaze of windows,
noses to the ground.
You go down the promenade, facing the sea
on this day of rain, this day of fire,
when a fusillade of castanets
shakes out the stitches of this
tightly woven plot of hour on hour on hour.

It is the call of another orbit:
follow it, go down to the horizon,
impending, overhung
by a lead-grey waterspout, a twister
more restless than the waves it spirals over,
a long salt whirlwind, whirlpooled to the clouds.
You must go down to where your feet
squeak on the wet shingle, catch
in the tangle of seaweed: this
is the moment, perhaps,
the long-awaited moment
that will save you from the end of your journey,
your days like links in a chain – motionless
progress, Arsenio, the familiar
frenzy of paralysis.

Listen: among the palm-trees
the tremulous stream of violin music
drowned, as it begins, by the thunder's
rolling iron drum.
The storm is at its sweetest
when the white eye of the Dog Star
blinks open in the brief blue
and the evening seems so distant
though it's coming soon enough;
lightning etches the sky, branching sudden
through the blushing light
like some tree of precious metal;
listen: the rumble of the gypsy drums . . .

Go down into the hurled, headlong dark
that's turned this noon into a night of lit globes
swaying down the shore –
                    and out there, where sky and sea
are all one shadow, slow fishing boats pulse
with acetylene –
                    till anxious drops
start from the heavy sky, and the earth
steams as it drinks it down, and you
and the world around have rain
lapping at your ankles; drenched awnings flag
and flap; you hear nothing but the giant shearing
hiss of water hitting the ground, the wheeze
of hundreds of paper lanterns
crumpling on the street.

And so, lost among the sodden mats and wickerwork,
you are a reed that drags its roots behind you;
they cling so tight you'll never be free;
trembling with life, you can only stretch out
to a ringing emptiness of swallowed grief;
the crest of that old wave rolls you,
overwhelms you again,
everything that can reclaim you
does – street and porch and walls and mirrors – all
lock you in with the frozen myriad dead;
and if you feel the brush of some gesture,
the breath of a word,
that, Arsenio,
might be the sign – in this dissolving hour –
of a strangled life that rose for you; the wind
carrying it off with the ashes of the stars.

DRESS REHEARSALS

On the final evening
headlights swarm down the hill like lava
making brief beds
of moving embers you can almost hear
the night extinguishing.
Darkness slides over itself, drawing down
each of its blinds, then, hours later
– even more slowly –
opening them, and the world returns
as a slur of ash and rumour, birds
calling out their names to themselves,
repeating their lines in their grey and hidden rooms.

How many more days of twilight, nightfall, dawn?
How many seasons flicked through
like frames in a ciné-film,
till the loose celluloid spins
tickering on the spool? The summers stall
in the machine and burn up;
winter is a white wall.
Years lurch,
untangling: the fast-forward trees
sprawl, in a week, from bud-burst to leaf-fall.
How much more of this life and death,
and these, their beautiful endless dress rehearsals?

EASTER, LIGURIA

Another day watching the ocean move
under the sun; pines, wisteria, lemon trees.
I darken this paradise like a sudden wind:
olive leaves, blown on their backs, silver
to razor-wire; cameras click in the wall.

Everyone is going home, and I realise
I have no idea what that means.
I listen to the shrieking of the gulls
and try to remember. How long ago
did I notice that the light was wrong,
that something inside me was broken?
Standing here, feeling nothing at all.
How long have I been leaving?
I don't know.

WIDOW'S WALK

On the *passeggiata*,
on the rocks
at the Marinella Bar again,
losing what remains of my language
to a thickening rain,
a week of rain
that's almost stopped the sea.
Trying to escape myself,
but there's always
someone
wanting to sew my shadow back.
The fisherman on his rock
under the red flags
has two fish in his bucket
swimming nowhere, side by side.
Lines of lacquered beetles
are rowing boats
turned upside-down;
the sea, mother-of-pearl
and broken shells;
the furled parasols
Madonnas in their shrouds.
I walk here
amongst the very old;
we watch the paint
flake from the hotel walls
and I take note, once again,
of the sign spelt out in English:

BATHING IN NOT SURE
FOR LACK OF RESCUE SERVIGE.
I felt like going in,
there and then,
like a widow
toppling forward at the grave;
going in after myself.

DIVING

The sudden sea is bright
and soundless: a changed channel
of dashed colour, scrolling
plankton, sea-darts, the slope
and loom of ghosts, something
slow and grey
sashaying through a school
of cobalt blue,
thin chains of silver fish
that link and spill and flicker away.

The elements imitate each other:
water-light playing on these stones
becomes a shaking flame; sunlight
stitches the rock-weed's rust and green,
swaying, sea-wavering; one red
twist scatters a shoal like a dust of static
– a million tiny shocks of white
dissolving in the lower depths.
The only sound
is the sea's mouth and the ticking
of the many mouths
that feed within it, sipping the light.

Dreaming high over the sea-forest
– the sea-bed green as a forest floor –
through the columns of gold
and streams of water-weed,
above a world in thrall,

charting by light
as a plane might glide,
slowly, silently
over woods in storm.

ABANDON

That moment, when the sun ignites the valley and picks out
every bud that's greened that afternoon; when birds
spill from the trees like shaken sheets; that sudden loosening
into beauty; the want in her eyes, her eyes' fleet blue;
the medals of light on water; the way the water intrigued
about her feet, the ocean walking her out into its depth,
sea lighting the length of her from the narrow waist
to the weight of the breasts; the way she lifted her eyes to me
and handed me back, simplified; that moment
at the end, knowing the one I had abandoned was myself,
edging with the sun around the bay's scoop of rocks,
rolling the last gold round the glass; that shelving love
as the sun was lost to us and the sky bruised, and the
stones grew cold as the shells on the beach at Naxos.

AT ROANE HEAD

for John Burnside

You'd know her house by the drawn blinds –
by the cormorants pitched on the boundary wall,
the black crosses of their wings hung out to dry.
You'd tell it by the quicken and the pine that hid it
from the sea and from the brief light of the sun,
and by Aonghas the collie, lying at the door
where he died: a rack of bones like a sprung trap.

A fork of barnacle geese came over, with that slow
squeak of rusty saws. The bitter sea's complaining pull
and roll; a whicker of pigeons, lifting in the wood.

She'd had four sons, I knew that well enough,
and each one wrong. All born blind, they say,
slack-jawed and simple, web-footed,
rickety as sticks. Beautiful faces, I'm told,
though blank as air.
Someone saw them once, outside, hirpling
down to the shore, chittering like rats,
and said they were fine swimmers,
but I would have guessed at that.

Her husband left her: said
they couldn't be his, they were more
fish than human,
said they were beglamoured,
and searched their skin for the showing marks.

For years she tended each difficult flame:
their tight, flickering bodies.
Each night she closed
the scales of their eyes to smoor the fire.

Until he came again,
that last time,
thick with drink, saying
he'd had enough of this,
all this witchery,
and made them stand
in a row by their beds,
twitching. Their hands
flapped; herring-eyes
rolled in their heads.
He went along the line
relaxing them
one after another
with a small knife.

It's said she goes out every night to lay
blankets on the graves to keep them warm.
It would put the heart across you, all that grief.

There was an otter worrying in the leaves, a heron
loping slow over the water when I came
at scraich of day, back to her door.

She'd hung four stones in a necklace, wore
four rings on the hand that led me past the room
with four small candles burning

which she called 'the room of rain'.
Milky smoke poured up from the grate
like a waterfall in reverse
and she said my name
and it was the only thing
and the last thing that she said.

She gave me a skylark's egg in a bed of frost;
gave me twists of my four sons' hair; gave me
her husband's head in a wooden box.
Then she gave me the sealskin, and I put it on.

HAMMERSMITH WINTER

It is so cold tonight; too cold for snow,
and yet it snows. Through the drawn curtain
shines the snowlight I remember as a boy,
sitting up at the window watching it fall.
But you're not here, now, to lead me back
to bed. None of you are. Look at the snow,
I said, to whoever might be near, I'm cold,
would you hold me. Hold me. Let me go.

NOTES & ACKNOWLEDGEMENTS

Silvered Water: placing a silver coin in a bowl of water or throwing it into a well is a traditional Scottish blessing, or preparation for a wish.

Signs on a White Field
sun-cups: hollows in ice caused by surface melting during intense sunshine.
snow penitents: pinnacles or spikes of compacted snow or ice caused by partial ablation of an ice field exposed to the sun.

By Clachan Bridge
stone-baby: the medical term is *lithopedion*; this occurs when a foetus dies during an ectopic pregnancy, is too large to be reabsorbed by the body, and calcifies.

The Plague Year
observatory: the Griffith Observatory in Los Angeles was the scene of the knife fight in *Rebel Without a Cause* (1955).
Pere Marquette: pronounced 'peer'.

A Gift
dwayberries: deadly nightshade – a poison, as are all the plants mentioned.

Strindberg in Berlin
Strindberg took a flat in Berlin in the autumn of 1892 and became a regular at *Zum schwarzen Ferkel*, where he first encountered Munch, Hamsun and the Polish writer and musician Stanisław Przybyszewski. During his brief stay in

the city he met, and became engaged to, Frida Uhl, while
conducting an affair with a young Norwegian, Dagny Juel.
Strindberg and Munch were rivals for Juel's attentions, but
she married Przybyszewski. It was around this time that
Strindberg's lifelong interest in alchemy began.
mareld: (Swedish) sea-fire, also known in English as
'seasparkle': the phenomenon of bioluminescence,
where high concentrations of plankton (*Noctiluca scintillans*)
containing an enzyme called luciferas give off light
when disturbed.

Tinsel
tinsel: the losing of something; the sustaining of harm, damage
or detriment; loss.

Leaving St Kilda
This describes an anti-clockwise circumnavigation of the main
island, Hirta, then Soay, followed by a clockwise turn around
Boreray.

Kalighat
the Kali Temple, Kolkata.

Pentheus and Dionysus
from *Metamorphoses*, Book III.

The Daughters of Minyas
from *Metamorphoses*, Book IV.

Ode to a Large Tuna in the Market
'Oda a un Gran Atún en el Mercado' from *Odas Elementales*.

Albatross in Co. Antrim
'L'Albatros' from *Les fleurs du mal*.

The Great Midwinter Sacrifice, Uppsala
suggested by Adam of Bremen's *Gesta Hammaburgensis Ecclesiae Pontificum* (*History of the Archbishops of Hamburg-Bremen*, translated by Francis J. Tschan, New York, 1959).

The Hammam
Cağaloğlu Hamami, Istanbul.

Unspoken Water: running water taken from under a bridge (over which the living pass and the dead are carried) and collected in a vessel that should not be allowed to touch the ground. It must be brought in the dawn or twilight to the house of the sick or bewitched person, and carried in complete silence. A wooden ladle containing a piece of silver is dipped in and the victim given three sips of the 'silvered' water. The remainder is then sprinkled over and around the body, or poured into a corner stone of the building or behind the fire-flag, naming the afflicted person. If the stone splits the illness or curse is fatal. In Scotland this is traditionally regarded as a powerful charm against the Evil Eye and for healing the sick.

The Wood of Lost Things
docken suit: a suit made of dock leaves.

Calling Home
'Hemåt' from *Sanningsbarriären*; this free version was included in *The Deleted World* (Enitharmon Press, 2006).

Ictus
ictus: metrical stress; the beat of the pulse; a stroke, seizure.
cack-handed: clumsy / left-handed.

The Unwritten Letter
'Su una lettera non scritta' from *La Bufera e Altro*.

During Dinner
Hawthorn flowers contain trimethylamine, one of the first chemicals formed when body tissue starts to decay, with an odour also said to be reminiscent of the sexual secretions of aroused women.

Arsenio
'Arsenio' from *Ossi di Seppia*.

Widow's Walk
the widow's walk: a high coastal walk or platform where fishermen's wives waited for sight of the returning boats.

At Roane Head
quicken: the rowan.

Acknowledgements are due to the editors
of the following:

*Archipelago, The Atlantic, Birtan í Húminu, Brick, Granta,
Guardian, Little Star, London Review of Books, Manhattan Review,
New Writing 15, New York Review of Books, Poetry, Poetry Ireland
Review, Poetry London, Poetry Review, Spectator, Times Literary
Supplement.*

'Ictus' was commissioned by Carol Ann Duffy for *Answering
Back* (Picador); 'Dress Rehearsals' was published in *Raising the
Iron* (Cargo Press) edited by David Harsent.

The latter stages of the writing of this book were supported by
a welcome grant from the National Lottery through Arts
Council England. I am also hugely grateful for the time spent
at the Liguria Study Center at Bogliasco and, once again, at the
Santa Maddalena Foundation in Donnini.